D0529569

DIGITAL AND INFORMATION LITERACY ™

CREATING CONTENT
MAXIMIZING WIKIS, WIDGETS, BLOGS, AND MORE

J. ELIZABETH MILLS

rosen publishing's
rosen central®

New York

To cyber-wise tweens and teens everywhere—may you tread carefully, treat each other well, and make the Internet one rockin' creative space!

Published in 2011 by The Rosen Publishing Group, Inc.
29 East 21st Street, New York, NY 10010

Copyright © 2011 by The Rosen Publishing Group, Inc.

First Edition

All rights reserved. No part of this book may be reproduced in any form without permission in writing from the publisher, except by a reviewer.

Library of Congress Cataloging-in-Publication Data

Mills, J. Elizabeth.
Creating content: maximizing wikis, widgets, blogs, and more / J. Elizabeth Mills.—1st ed.
    p. cm.—(Digital and information literacy)
Includes bibliographical references and index.
ISBN 978-1-4488-1322-3 (lib. bdg.)
ISBN 978-1-4488-2293-5 (pbk.)
ISBN 978-1-4488-2299-7 (6-pack)
1. User-generated content—Juvenile literature. 2. Social media—Juvenile literature. 3. Web 2.0—Juvenile literature. 4. Internet and teenagers—Juvenile literature. 5. Internet—Safety measures—Juvenile literature. I. Title.
ZA4482.M55 2011
006.7—dc22

2010026860

Manufactured in the United States of America

CPSIA Compliance Information: Batch #W11YA: For further information, contact Rosen Publishing, New York, New York, at 1-800-237-9932.

CONTENTS

INTRODUCTION

Think of all the ways you use the Internet in your daily life. The Web has become a public scrapbook, filing cabinet, music player, movie theater, and vast encyclopedia all in one. People live their lives online now, making plans on Evite, catching up with friends on Facebook, sharing the latest viral video on YouTube, and commenting on photos of a friend's birthday party on Flickr.

Time is measured in instants. You can communicate with friends and family via e-mail, instant messaging (IM), or webcam no matter where you live. Dozens of Web pages on a research topic pop up with the click of a mouse. Communities now extend farther than ever before, offering new opportunities for members to learn from each other and improve society.

Information is all around us. But not all information is reliable. Web sites are created every day, some with little expertise. You need to develop a filter to critically analyze the amount of data you encounter daily. Ask questions to understand which sites are reputable, how to cite online articles, and how to ask for permission to use copyrighted material. Respecting others' work by giving credit is always the right thing to do.

The world is changing at a dizzying speed. It's no longer enough just to know how to navigate the Internet—you must also understand how to guard your privacy as social networking sites update and modify

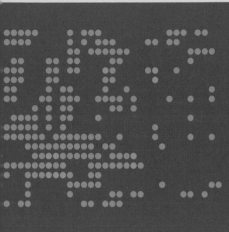

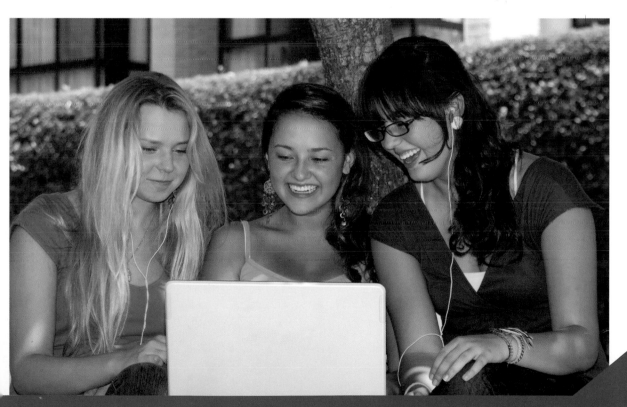

The Internet is a great place to share your favorite photos, music, videos, Web sites, and other media with your friends and discover new artists.

their settings. Who can access your personal information? What can you do to protect yourself? How much should people know about you and your life?

The good news is that you can be in control of your identity on the Internet. Generate your own online content through blogs and Web sites. Upload images and give feedback on everything you see and hear around you. Socialize and express yourself through social media. And choose to turn off and delete programs that use your information inappropriately. As you discover how to play, learn, and interact with others online, remember that the Internet is a public space. Always ask yourself whether you want strangers, classmates, or teachers to see what you're posting. Good conduct and respectful behavior are rewarded in this new online community.

Chapter 1

You, Online

What makes you who you are? Is it the clothes you wear, the music you listen to, or your hairstyle? How would you describe yourself using your own words in a journal or diary? Who will you be online? Who is your online audience?

Blogs

Once, the Internet was a collection of information—news, weather, and sports sites with scores and statistics. Today, the Internet is referred to as Web 2.0, and it has become a place for user-generated content—thoughts, opinions, and media created and uploaded by users to express themselves in all kinds of ways. Instead of being faced with unlimited information, you control the content you read and share. There is now a whole new online space where you can create a completely different identity. One place to do this is on a blog.

A blog is an online diary or journal. The word "blog" is a combination of the words "Web log." Bloggers write posts about anything and everything. Some blogs are highly personal and talk about friendship,

You can learn about starting a blog, creating compelling content, publicizing your site, and making money by attending workshops and discussions led by industry professionals.

relationships, parents, or teachers. Other blogs focus on broader themes, such as news, food, travel, or music.

A blogger usually updates his or her site regularly with new entries. And these entries typically appear in reverse chronological order, with the newest post at the top of the page. A blog may consist of only text, or a combination of text, images, and video for a multimedia experience.

How Do You Begin Blogging?

There are several Web sites that have ready-made blog templates. Blogger is a site popular for its simple template. Other services include Xanga, WordPress, and LiveJournal.

Choose the name of your blog, pick a background design, and then fill in your bio, background information, and the "philosophy" of your blog.

One important field is the Blog Archive. Since posts are listed with the newest entry first, older posts are organized by year, then by month, and then by post name in the archive, allowing readers to go back and find an older post.

What to Write About

Once you set up your blog, what do you write about? According to some statistics, there are more than one hundred million blogs out there. How do you distinguish yourself? Think back to the question at the beginning of this chapter—what makes you who you are? Write about what interests you, using your own words and unique style. Keep your posts brief, and soon you'll have a blog that other people will want to follow.

Where Are Your Readers?

A popular and unique feature of blogs is the comments section, where readers can post their thoughts. Bloggers rely on this immediate feedback to stay in touch and fuel their writing.

It's great to receive comments from your readers. And if you want to keep your blog fresh, respond to them. Since the Internet is a public place, you should always be thoughtful and considerate about what you write. If you do, your readers will respect you and enjoy having a dialogue with you. They'll come back to read posts and leave comments because they feel you care about their opinions. You should screen the comments that appear on your site in case any of them are inappropriate.

Post frequently—if there's nothing new to read, people will leave your blog and find something else. The world is moving quickly—you need to capture people's attention immediately. It's also a good idea to set up RSS feeds on your blog. These enable your readers to subscribe to your blog and receive posts either in their e-mail inbox or on a news reader, such as Bloglines or Google Reader.

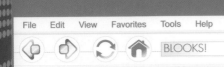

File   Edit   View   Favorites   Tools   Help

BLOOKS!

Blooks!

Books have been the inspiration for many a blog, but did you know that blogs can become books? A book that comes from an online blog is called a blook. A famous example of a blook that then became a movie in 2009 is *Julie & Julia*. Blogs have a free-form and personal writing style—one that is not always easy to translate into books. But sometimes a great book idea can come from an unusual blog.

Comment on other people's blogs, too. Start a conversation that will help build your readership.

Web Sites, Widgets, Wikis, and Twitter

Another way to develop an identity on the Web is with a Web site. Similar to a blog, a Web site is usually designed as a go-to spot for people to learn about you and your interests.

A Web site is a network of pages and multimedia connected and filed under a common URL, or uniform resource locator. A URL is what you type into your Internet browser to find a particular Web page. HTML, or hypertext markup language, is used to create and design Web pages.

Like blogs, Web sites can be about anything and everything. Major news sites have Web sites; businesses use Web sites to sell their goods; and people create personal Web sites to share information and photos with family members. Some Web sites have no purpose at all except to be entertaining.

Widgets

Have you ever looked on a Web site and seen a scrolling number, weather forecast, news ticker, or clock? These are called widgets—tools meant to provide extra information on various topics. Widgets allow viewers to scan a Web page and pick up a little information here and there—perfect for today's multitasking world. iGoogle is a customizable portal or gateway page that is made up of widgets—you can move them around, add and delete them, and keep the ones you like best.

Many blogs include widgets in the form of lists, such as Books I'm Reading, Music I Like, and Blogs I Follow. You might consider including them on your blog to give your readers more ways to identify with you and bring

Many television channels use Web-based widgets to enhance their media coverage, deepen viewers' knowledge of particular topics, and maintain constant access to information.

readers to your blog. When you connect with other bloggers, they are more likely to connect with you.

Wikis

A wiki is a collection of pages on a particular topic with content that can be modified by its users. Wikis rely on their contributors to check and verify the information. Changes to a wiki page are recorded in a section called Recent Changes, which logs all the additions. Creators can view earlier versions of the pages and manage corrections.

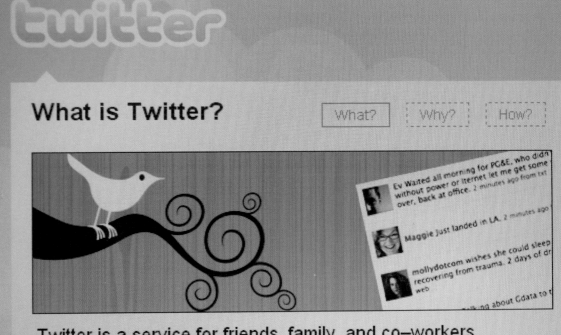

Twitter (http://www.twitter.com) was created in 2006 to allow people to communicate using text messages. By August 2010, twenty billion tweets had been posted.

Twitter

Twitter is a microblogging service in which you express yourself in short "tweets" of 140 characters. The posts appear in real time, so your followers receive a minute-by-minute log of your day.

The two simplest parts of Twitter etiquette are the "retweet" and the "hashtag." A retweet is a reposting of a tweet. Twitter encourages people to create networks of followers. When you tweet, the post goes out to your network. If someone else likes that tweet and wants to share it with their network, they retweet it by copying your post and typing "RT" in front of it. Now your tweet has reached an even greater number of people. The hashtag or "#" symbol groups relevant tweets together under one heading. If you were to group all the tweets about the Twilight series, the hashtag would look like "#twilight." The hashtag for the video game *Halo* would be "#halo."

TEN GREAT QUESTIONS

TO ASK AN INFORMATION EXPERT

1. How do I access my library's research databases?

2. Where do I look for citation information on a Web page?

3. How do I avoid coming across X-rated Web sites?

4. How do I know if the section of a video I want to use is covered by fair use?

5. What is Web 2.0?

6. What are some ways to interact with people on social networking sites?

7. How do I let people know I started a blog?

8. How do I submit a correction to a Wikipedia page?

9. Should I have a Web site, a blog, or both?

10. How do I find out what my school's policy is on cyberbullying?

Chapter 2

Your Words Online

The social nature of Web 2.0 extends beyond personal Web sites and blogs. Information is constantly being created, shared, modified, and improved by a vast network of people. News stations often rely on the Internet for interesting stories that are circulating around the blogosphere—the world of blogs.

Sometimes the TV shows you watch will display a banner at the bottom of the screen that directs you to the show's Web site for a deeper look at a particular topic. There is so much information out there and so many ways to access it. How do you take part?

Wikipedia

Let's say you have to write a report on whales. Type "whales" into Yahoo! or Google, hit the "Search" button, and what do you find? Page after page of links to all kinds of sites—marine biology programs, photographs, museums, and Wikipedia entries. What is Wikipedia?

Jimmy Wales *(shown here)* and Larry Sanger launched Wikipedia as a collaborative information collection in 2001. In 2007, a mobile phone application was created, further widening the site's audience.

Wikipedia is an online encyclopedia of content compiled by people who want to share information about topics that interest them. People all around the world come together to create entries on just about every topic you can think of. The information is often generated by people with specific expertise or training. Wikipedia is also a valuable resource for information on popular culture, since it is constantly being updated.

Reliable or Not?

Anyone can write an entry and publish it for others to read. But it is peer-reviewed, so if there are any errors in the entry, another user will often come along and fix them. But before the entry gets fixed, you may put some incorrect information into your report.

The next time you're on Wikipedia, look at the top of the page. You may see a box saying the page has unverified information or lacks cited sources. This is one of the main reasons why teachers and librarians do not approve of Wikipedia as a research source. They prefer that students use print journals and encyclopedias, or academic work. Print materials have usually been carefully reviewed and checked by experts.

File   Edit   View   Favorites   Tools   Help

SOCIAL SITES

Social Sites

Not all social networking communities are alike. Some focus on a particular topic. Digg.com is a news site to which people send links to interesting stories and comment on them. Digg appeals to competitive people who want to be the first to "break" a story. Yelp.com is a neighborhood site with user-generated reviews of restaurants, shopping, cultural events, and other aspects of life in various cities across the country. Delicious is a site centered around posting and sharing online bookmarks.

Wikipedia, on the other hand, has only its own users, and they cannot read every page. There are fifteen million entries in more than two hundred languages. The Web site was created with the philosophy that open sharing of information is important in Web 2.0, and approval from peers would encourage good behavior on the part of the contributors.

Using Wikipedia

Does this mean you can't use Wikipedia at all? No, but it does mean you have to be careful about what you read. Use Wikipedia only as an initial resource to learn some basic facts about a topic. Then scroll down the page to the reference list. These usually include print materials you can find at a library or even through a Google Books search to get information that has been reviewed and checked. And you can cite those sources, or other reliable sources, in your bibliography. Just make sure you check them out first!

Do the same for Web sites such as About.com, Answers.com, Blurtit.com, Yahoo! Answers, and others. Good researchers always view their online sources with a critical eye. Ask these questions as you read—who is the author of this information? What is his or her level of expertise on the subject? Can this information be found elsewhere as well? Is the material current? Does the article have a bias? Is there a better resource available? Answers to these questions will help guide you in your research. Always be sure that your research is coming from legitimate sources.

To cite online articles in your bibliography, list the author's name—last name first—the title of the article in quotations, the name of the Web site or organization, the publication date, and the URL in brackets. If there is no publication date, you can put the date you found on the Web site instead. This is called the retrieval date. You can go to certain Web sites like NoodleTools (http://www.noodletools.com) for more information about citing sources.

Technology has enabled Facebook users to access their accounts anywhere at any time, via handheld devices. Now, you can change your status anytime you want.

Social Networking

Web 2.0 is about creating and maintaining a community in every aspect of life as quickly and currently as possible. The up-to-the-minute nature of Twitter and social networks has accelerated online interaction. What's going on in your head? Post it!

Facebook, MySpace, and More

Whether it's Club Penguin, Whyville!, Dgamer, MySpace, or Facebook, chances are you're using some kind of social networking site. According to a recent study by DoubleClick Performics, a search marketing company, 83 percent of kids ages ten to fourteen spend more than an hour a day on the Internet, and 72 percent of kids are on some kind of social networking site.

These sites offer a customizable space where users can express their interests, background, thoughts, or ideas and receive feedback from friends. Similar to blogging, one of the most attractive aspects of social networking is commenting. Here in cyberspace, friendships are made and broken, reshaped and strengthened. Groups form around common interests or common dislikes, as users "friend" each other.

My Social Network

As with blogs and Web sites, you can design your own page on many social networks. Include as much or as little information as you like. Add applications with games or polls, take quizzes, and post profile photos. Your online identity allows you to perform and show off for friends. These networks are about self-branding—you are in charge of your identity. The anonymity of the Internet and the ease with which you can create new profiles makes trying to be someone else appealing. Simply make up a new screen name or create a new profile. Upload a different photo or icon, and you can be a new person online. Some sites even allow you to choose an avatar—a visual representation of yourself.

You can create avatars for social networking sites, video games, online role-playing games, IM sites, and other places on the Internet. Avatars can even be animated.

How to Get Started

Browse around the different sites. Make sure you're using one that's right for your age group. Read over the terms of use with an adult so that both of you understand the rules and restrictions. Then invite your friends to join. Send friend requests and begin your network. Set up any widgets or media you want on your page. Then post your thoughts and comment on others' posts. And remember to always be thoughtful and considerate in everything you write online.

Chapter 3

Your Image Online

With the proliferation of digital cameras, everyone is taking photos and videos of everything, including themselves, all the time. Flickr and YouTube are two of the most popular sites for sharing visual media, but there are many others, each with its own specialty.

Photos

Flickr is a content management Web site that offers to host your pictures on a basic account for free. You can edit the photos, organize them, drop them onto maps to assign locations, make cards and books and other things featuring your photos, and keep in touch with your friends and family through their comments and tags.

Tags

Flickr and other sites create communities through an organizational system known as tagging. Tags are keywords or phrases that describe a photo,

It's fun to take all kinds of photos of friends and family members, but you should always back up your files to keep your media library safe.

blog posting, video, or online bookmark. Tags are a way to file these separate items under one searchable topic. As a result, people who might otherwise have nothing in common can meet and discuss a blog post about the presidential election or a collection of whale photos just by searching those tags.

On Flickr, you can do a search to find all the photos that have the same tag. For instance, if you are looking for photos of dogs, search using the word "dogs." If you click on "Popular Tags," you come to a cluster of words known as a tag cloud. This is a visual representation of the popular tags on the site and the level of their popularity. The words that appear in a larger, bold font are the tags that have been used the most. Conversely, the tinier words have been used the least. When you create your own tags, try using unusual words—you're more likely to stand out as a result.

You can create clouds from regular text, too. The next time you write a report for school, copy and paste some of your text into Wordle (http://www.wordle.net). You'll be amazed by what you see. Tag clouds give you a clear idea of which words you overuse and what your main points are. The clouds are visually appealing as well.

Videos

Named "Invention of the Year" by *Time* magazine in 2006, YouTube is the second most-searched Web site on the Internet after its parent company, Google. YouTube features clips of movies, TV shows, vintage commercials, amateur performances, vlogs (video blogs), and film students' productions. When a particularly popular video is sent bouncing around from inbox to inbox and from Twitter feed to blog post, it's known as a viral video.

The New Television?

Complete with big, beautiful, high-resolution screens and perpetual access to streaming TV shows and movies, home computers are turning into interactive televisions.

YouTube's goal is to take back a few of the almost five hours a day spent by the average American in front of the television by continuously teasing viewers with more and more videos to watch.

When you set up an account with YouTube, you create a favorites list made up of videos you like best and want to watch in the future. You can also make customized playlists.

When you've finished viewing a video, you can rate it by clicking "Like" or "Dislike" and leave comments for the videographer. Like everything in Web 2.0, comments are key—they provide immediate feedback about

Some television networks have partnered with YouTube to connect with viewers and enable them to participate in important events. During this presidential debate, people ask the candidates questions using the video site.

what you liked or didn't like and how to make the video better. And, as always, diplomacy is the best policy when giving criticism.

Search Tips

To find videos to watch, you have several options. You can click on one of the suggestions to the right of the video box, use the search option, or browse. To do a search, type a tag or a category into the search box at the top of the page. To browse, you click the browse button and choose the category or channel. A channel is a group of uploaded videos.

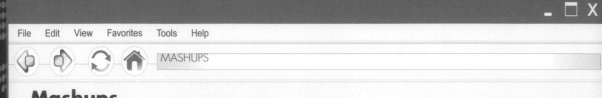

File   Edit   View   Favorites   Tools   Help

MASHUPS

Mashups

Have you ever seen a video on YouTube in which the video and audio didn't quite match up? Chances are you were watching a mashup—a video overlaid with separate audio, original content mixed with existing material. Incredibly popular on the Internet today, mashups are becoming a new form of media. In the same way that teens make up new identities on social networks, people are taking content from everywhere and creating hybrid content. This trend is causing a lot of debate and concern over copyright and fair use.

Categories are listed on the left side of the page. You can also browse the most popular videos, the videos being watched now, and other groups.

Sharing Tips

One of the best ways to participate in the YouTube community is to post videos of your own. Perhaps you have some home movies or amateur performances you want to share. Three important things to keep in mind when shooting a video for YouTube:

- Keep it short—ten minutes maximum.
- Use good lighting and sound equipment.
- Make sure your content is new and fresh.

There are too many videos on too few topics—make yours stand out by being creative and saying something unique.

Rely on your unique personality and creativity to make interesting videos. If you show your life as you see it, viewers will connect with your material and with you.

Once you've uploaded your videos, you can choose to allow or disallow viewers' comments and ratings, share the videos over e-mail, and enable other people to embed your videos on their social networking sites and blogs. Like Flickr, YouTube has a widget you can install on your Web site or blog to enable YouTube capability.

Chapter 4

What to Watch Out For

The Internet is full of exciting ways to express yourself and be part of an immense community. But the Internet is a public space—as public as your local park, mall, or beach. Whatever you do can be viewed by your classmates, teachers, parents, school administrators, and future employers, as well as complete strangers.

Internet: Public and Private

Unfortunately, online communities often contain members who want to cause trouble or hurt others through their words and actions. Even though the networks and Web pages you share with your friends may seem private, strangers need only a search engine to find you using blog posts about your personal details.

Here are some ways to stay safe:

- If you have a blog, tell your parents about it so that they can help you monitor your readers.

Tread carefully on the Web. You may one day be evaluated by teachers, school administrators, college admissions officers, and future employers based on your online profile and actions.

- If you receive any inappropriate or hurtful comments, share them with a grown-up.
- If you decide to put pictures online, show them to an adult who can help you weed out images that might cause trouble.

In general, if you wouldn't put up the picture in your school hallway, don't post it online. Keep all of your personal information—your full name, address, phone number—private.

The Dark Side

Sites with inappropriate content thrive on the Internet. They hide behind malicious software that can take over a computer and make it difficult to close browser windows. As computers become more and more common in classrooms at school, you may encounter these sites at some point while doing research or checking e-mail. If you come across an inappropriate site, close your browser and tell your teacher or another grown-up.

Cyberbullying

Diaries and journals have always been safe, private places where kids can work through all kinds of emotional roller coasters as they grow up and deal with pressures at home and at school. Often the harsh and sad words that appear there are just temporary thunderstorms in otherwise calm lives.

But in the case of blogs, these thoughts are no longer private. Anyone can find and read them, and pass them along to others. Grudges, breakups, and rivalries are spilled onto an online page that might as well be taped to the outside of your locker at school.

What Is It?

Cyberbullying involves sending any sort of text message, instant message, post, or e-mail to hurt and harass the recipient. Posting rumors or embarrassing photos, outing someone's secret to others, and threatening physical harm are all forms of cyberbullying.

These messages can be anonymous or signed; they can threaten or mock; but they are all meant to hurt. A cyberbully may even gather a gang to collectively harass another student.

Cyberbullying creates feelings of depression, fear, and extremely low self-esteem. Recipients of hate mail feel alone, thinking no one else understands or can help them. They may feel as if there's no one to turn to.

The best way to resolve a dispute is face-to-face, not hidden away online. Find a grown-up who can help you through a difficult situation in a healthy, constructive way.

According to a recent survey by Pew Internet & American Life Project, about one-third of American teens, about thirteen million people, say they've been victims of cyberbullying. Girls seem to be targets more than boys are. And about half of the teens who spend time on MySpace and Facebook encounter cyberbullying.

Why Does It Happen?

In some cases, kids aren't thinking about the fact that the Internet is public. They send a hurtful text to some friends, and in a few hours it's flown around school. In other cases, kids know full well the impact of their actions. They exploit the viral nature of the Internet to do their work for them.

File   Edit   View   Favorites   Tools   Help

SEXTING

Sexting

According to a recent study, about one in five teens has sent, received, or forwarded a sext—a text message with sexually suggestive photos. More than a third of the teens know someone who has sent a sext, and while these are usually sent to friends or boyfriends or girlfriends, occasionally teens send sexts to strangers. This is a dangerous practice no matter who the photos are being sent to. They are an invasion of privacy and highly inappropriate, objectifying the person in the photo and sending the wrong signal. The best thing to do is delete these messages and stop the forwarding chain. If sexts have no audience, they have no reason to be sent.

Hiding behind a computer screen, anyone can become a cyberbully. It's easier to type in the privacy of your own home than it is to face up to someone and see their reaction.

Some studies show that kids who instigate cyberbullying have been on the receiving end as well, perpetuating the cycle of violence. A cyberbully enjoys hurting others because he or she doesn't have to deal with or focus on his or her own problems. Perhaps the bully thinks the harassment will make the victim stronger or teach him or her a lesson.

What Are the Consequences?

Bullies believe they can hide online by creating fake user names. However, they leave cyberfootprints that the police can use to trace their movements. The police take cyberbullying very seriously. They may contact the Internet service provider (ISP) to obtain the bully's home address and phone number.

If he or she is reported to the ISP multiple times for harassment, Internet service may be suspended or canceled. Fourteen states now have cyber-bullying laws to prosecute offenders, with more states considering them.

Some schools have started cyberbully awareness programs to warn students about the pain and harm they're causing and inform them of the punishments—in some cases, suspension or expulsion. The programs also let the victims know they're not alone, encouraging them to report any incidents. And social networking sites such as MySpace and Facebook are getting involved, too, providing tips on how to report abuse or harassment. If you are involved in cyber-bullying, they will terminate your account.

What Do I Do If It Happens to Me?

Reporting and speaking up are two of the biggest ways you can fight back. It may not be easy—you don't want to become the target. But if you don't stand up, who will? Put an end to the cycle and don't pass on hurtful or nasty messages or photos. Be friendly and

You may be pressured by classmates to participate in cyberbullying. But keep in mind the fact that you are not just hurting someone else, you're also hurting yourself.

supportive to victims of cyberbullying. And go online and sign the Megan Pledge against cyberbullying.

Be proactive: block the person who is harassing you. Delete the bully's address from your e-mail contact list. If he or she posts on your social networking page, delete the bully as a friend and remove his or her posts from your wall. Print and save any hurtful correspondence. You may need proof if the situation involves the police. Talk to a parent or school guidance counselor if the problem persists.

If you have been the bully, stop and think. Put yourself in the other person's shoes. Would you want someone to do that to you? How would that make you feel? Take a break if you are feeling really angry and out of control. When you get back to your computer, things may not seem so bad, and you will have avoided hurting someone else.

How to Stay Safe Online

The bottom line is this: if you ever read or see anything on the Internet that makes you feel uncomfortable or scared or upset, tell a grown-up, a parent, or a teacher. You've done nothing wrong—it's not your fault.

MYTHS&FACTS

MYTH I don't need to look at the privacy settings on my social networking profile page. Only my friends can see what I post.

FACT You should look at the privacy settings on your social networking site with a grown-up so that both of you understand how to keep you, and your media, safe.

MYTH Cyberbullying isn't as bad as regular bullying because it's not face-to-face.

FACT In some ways, cyberbullying is worse than face-to-face bullying because the victim can't confront his or her aggressor. Victims can't fight back or stand up for themselves. Instead, they face humiliation and shame when they come to school, knowing everyone has read or seen what the bully sent around to classmates.

MYTH I have some photos of myself that show me doing some things that could potentially get me in trouble. If I send them to my friends, no one else will see them.

FACT You never know what will happen to photos you send over the Internet. They could be snatched by someone hacking your account, your friends could turn on you and send them around school, or a bully at school could see the photos on a friend's phone and start a nasty rumor. It's better to keep compromising photos to yourself.

35

Chapter 5

What's Yours, What's Not

How do you protect your work online? How much of someone else's work can you legally use? Part of being a responsible member of Web 2.0 is knowing what's yours and what's not.

Copyright

Copyright is a law in the United States that protects the works of its citizens, whether they are artists, composers, writers, or anyone else who creates something. When you write a report or make a drawing for school, you automatically own the copyright for that work just by creating it. This means you

Whatever you create online—whether it's a Web site, blog, novel, or computerized portrait—you own the content. Make sure you know how to protect your material.

are the only one with the right to distribute it, make copies of it, perform it, display it, or adapt it in some way. Because the material is copyrighted, it cannot be used without the copyright owner's permission. That's you!

Infringement

Your whale report took you days to research and write. Then someone gets a hold of the file on your computer at school, prints it out, and turns it in as his or her own work. You would feel pretty cheated, wouldn't you? That person has taken something you created and called it his or her own. This is called copyright infringement.

Now think about the entertainment industry. What are your favorite movies, bands, or TV shows? Think about all the time and effort that went into those performances and how proud their creators must feel. If you post those performances on YouTube or on your blog without giving credit or asking permission, you're doing the same thing as the person who stole your report. Those performances aren't yours. They belong to the people who created them. By giving credit and asking permission, you are respecting these artists and showing appreciation for their creativity and talent.

Here are some guidelines:

- Don't upload entire movies or TV shows. While YouTube has gained notoriety and subscribers through its TV and movie content, in most cases that content was not obtained legally.
- Include only about 10 percent of other bloggers' material on your blog or Web site, give them credit, and link back to their blog so that your readers can find the whole article.
- Always cite your sources and make sure that your content is in your words.

As you can see, it's important to always be respectful of all content, even online content. Almost everything on the Web is copyrighted, even if you don't see the © symbol. So be sure to give credit where it's due.

What's Fair Use?

Copyright law does have certain limitations, one of which is called fair use. Under this doctrine, you can use a portion of a copyrighted work for education and research.

Courts look at the following questions to decide if someone's copyright has been violated:

1. Will the material be used for educational purposes?
2. Will only a small portion of the whole work be used?
3. Will use of the material keep the creator from making money?
4. Is the material being used for commercial or nonprofit purposes?

However, there is no clear rule to follow, so you're better off if you can avoid using copyrighted work.

What Can I Use?

The Smithsonian Institute gives students permission to use its content in school reports. There are other government Web sites that provide material to students as well. Always read the copyright statements and terms of use for everything you use.

Once you put your report up on the Internet, however, the rules change. People outside of your school can now access the information in your report, and it is no longer protected by the fair use doctrine. Now it's being used for more than just educational purposes.

Copyright protection does not always last forever. Works that are very old, such as Shakespeare's plays and many classical music pieces, are in the public domain—meaning you can use them and not pay for permission. However, you should always check to make sure a work is in the public domain first, and then always give credit.

If you want to use something that is copyrighted, find out the creator's name and send him or her a permissions letter or e-mail. You may have to

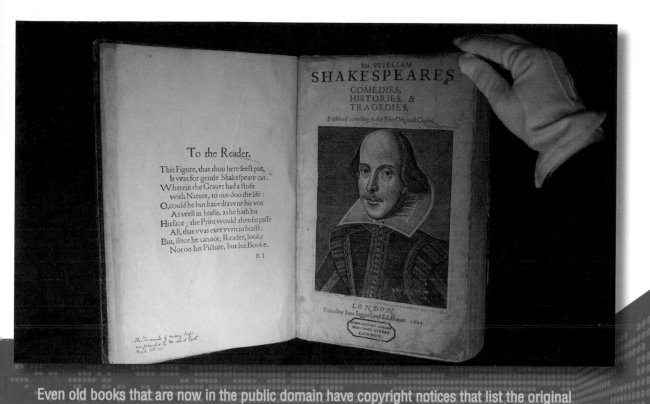

Even old books that are now in the public domain have copyright notices that list the original creator. Use the appropriate copyright notice to properly credit your sources.

pay a fee if the person says yes, but you will have done the right thing. Now you have the creator's authorization to use the work. If you receive no response, however, you do not automatically have the right to use the work just because you wrote a letter. You must have proof of consent.

How Do I Protect My Work?

Now that you know how to obtain approval to use someone else's work, let's look at how to protect your own work. As stated earlier, once you create something, it's yours—you own the copyright. So if you post it online, put a copyright line at the bottom of the page with the © symbol, the year, and your name. This lets people know the work belongs to you.

Privacy

Sites such as Flickr, Facebook, MySpace, and Blogger all have privacy settings that give you ways to restrict access to your information. YouTube, however, reserves the right to do whatever it wants with your videos, even though you hold the copyright. In addition, any other YouTube user may use your video without asking for your approval. This is an important issue to consider before uploading your work.

Creative Commons

If you want to enable people to share and embed your work on their blogs and Web sites, though, you should use a Creative Commons license. In our mashup culture, CC licenses do retain some rights for you but also release remixing rights to those who want to create new hybrid works legally. CC licenses help encourage a respectful sharing community.

There are many Web sites with licensed works that can be shared, remixed, or reused. Visit Creative Commons (http://www.search.creativecommons.org) for access to these sites.

The Last Word

The Internet can be an incredible place to share information and media and learn about new topics and events. But it has its dark side and limitations as well. You are in control of your actions online, so make sure you are always thoughtful and respectful in all you do, say, and share, and you will help make Web 2.0 a safer, more enjoyable place.

GLOSSARY

bias A personal judgment or opinion.

blog A Web site that contains an online personal journal with posts that appear in reverse chronological order.

blogosphere The online community of blogs.

copyright A U.S. law that protects the rights of people who create works such as music, books, and fine art.

cyberbullying Sending an e-mail, text message, or photo that will cause someone humiliation, anger, or shame.

embedding Putting a video on a Web page, blog, or social networking profile.

fair use A limitation to the copyright law that allows people to use a restricted portion of a copyrighted work without permission.

hashtag A symbol (#) that groups similar tweets.

mashup A hybrid of two different videos or one video and one audio file to make a new creative work.

portal A Web site made up of widgets, such as My.Yahoo.com and iGoogle.com.

privacy A person's freedom from intrusion.

retweet To share another person's tweet with your network.

RSS feed A way for readers to subscribe to a blog and receive updated posts in their e mail inbox or on a central news reader.

tag A keyword or phrase that categorizes an online bookmark, blog post, photo, or video.

tweet A post on Twitter that is restricted to 140 characters and is sent immediately.

widget A mini Web page that can be added to a Web site or blog to provide information or entertainment.

wiki An online information database that is created and modified by its users.

FOR MORE INFORMATION

Canada Safety Council
1020 Thomas Spratt Place
Ottawa, ON K1G 5L5
Canada
(613) 739-1535
Web site: http://safety-council.org
The Canada Safety Council provides tips for parents and rules for kids on
how to be safe in cyberspace.

Covenant House Nineline
(800) 999-9999
Web site: http://www.nineline.org
The Covenant House Nineline is a twenty-four-hour, toll-free crisis hotline that
provides crisis intervention, referral, and information services to home-
less, runaway, and other troubled youth and their families throughout
the United States.

Creative Commons
171 Second Street, Suite 300
San Francisco, CA 94105
(415) 369-8480
Web site: http://www.creativecommons.org
Creative Commons is a nonprofit corporation dedicated to making it easier
for people to share and build upon the work of others, consistent
with the rules of copyright. It provides free licenses and other legal
tools to mark creative work with the freedom the creator wants it to
carry so others can share, remix, use it commercially, or any combination thereof.

i-SAFE Inc.
500 Pasteur Court, Suite #100
Carlsbad, CA 92008
(760) 603-7911
Web site: http://www.isafe.org
i-Safe is the largest Internet safety Web site. It can be contacted with
    questions about its Web site, informational materials, student programs,
    and more.

Kinsa
Kinsa Headquarters
145 King Street West, 8th Floor
Toronto, ON M5H 1J8
Canada
(416) 682-5502
Web site: http://www.kinsa.net
Kinsa helps find, rescue, and heal children whose images are shared on
    the Internet.

Web Sites

Due to the changing nature of Internet links, Rosen Publishing has developed
an online list of Web sites related to the subject of this book. This site is
updated regularly. Please use this link to access the list:

http://www.rosenlinks.com/dil/maxi

FOR FURTHER READING

Ayers, Phoebe, Charles Matthews, Ben Yates. *How Wikipedia Works: And How You Can Be a Part of It*. San Francisco, CA: No Starch Press, 2008.

Boxer, Sarah. *Ultimate Blogs: Masterworks from the Wild Web*. New York, NY: Vintage Books, 2008.

Cindrich, Sharon. *A Smart Girl's Guide to the Internet: How to Connect with Friends, Find What You Need, and Stay Safe Online*. Middleton, WI: American Girl Publishing, 2009.

DeMott, Andrea, ed. *What Is the Impact of Cyberlife?* Detroit, MI: Greenhaven Press, 2008.

Gardner, Olivia, Emily Bruder, and Sarah Bruder. *Letters to a Bullied Girl*. New York, NY: Harper Paperbacks, 2008.

Jakubiak, David J. *A Smart Kid's Guide to Internet Privacy*. New York, NY: Rosen Publishing Group, 2010

Sande, Warren, and Carter Sande. *Hello World! Computer Programming for Kids and Other Beginners*. Greenwich, CT: Manning Publications, 2009.

Selfridge, Benjamin, Peter Selfridge, and Jennifer Osburn. *A Teen's Guide to Creating Web Pages and Blogs*. Waco, TX: Prufrock Press, 2009.

Willard, Nancy E. *Cyber-Safe Kids, Cyber-Savvy Teens: Helping Young People Learn to Use the Internet Safely and Responsibly*. San Francisco, CA: Jossey-Bass, 2007.

BIBLIOGRAPHY

Allman, Toney. *Mean Behind the Screen: What You Need to Know About Cyberbullying*. Mankato, MN: Compass Point Books, 2009.

Burrows, Terry. *Blogs, Wikis, MySpace, and More: Everything You Want to Know About Using Web 2.0 But Were Afraid to Ask*. Chicago, IL: Chicago Review Press, 2008.

Copyright Society of the U.S.A. "What Is Copyright?" April 5, 2010 (http://www.copyrightkids.org/whatcopyframes.htm).

Cox Communications in Partnership with the National Center for Missing & Exploited Children (NCMEC) and John Walsh. *Teen Online & Wireless Safety Survey: Cyberbullying, Sexting, and Parental Controls*. Atlanta, GA: May 2009.

Goodstein, Anastasia. *Totally Wired: What Teens and Tweens Are Really Doing Online*. New York, NY: St. Martin's Press, 2007.

Kids Health. "Internet Safety." September 2008 (http://kidshealth.org/parent/positive/family/net_safety.html).

Lenardon, John. *Protect Your Child on the Internet: A Parent's Toolkit*. Bellingham, WA: Self Counsel Press, 2006.

Miller, Michael. *You Tube 4 You*. Indianapolis, IN: Que Publishing, 2007.

Pew Research Center. *Pew Internet & American Life Project: PIP Cyberbullying Memo*. Washington, DC: June 27, 2007.

Rigby, Ben. *Mobilizing Generation 2.0: A Practical Guide to Using Web 2.0*. San Francisco, CA: Jossey-Bass, 2008.

University Laboratory High School. "Computer Literacy: Elements of Web Site Evaluation." April 15, 2010 (http://www.uni.illinois.edu/library/computerlit/evaluation.php).

INDEX

About the Author

J. Elizabeth Mills is a children's book author who spends way too much time on Facebook and Google Reader, dabbles with Twitter, and just can't quite commit to the regularity of a blog. But, overall, she thinks this Web 2.0 thing is pretty cool. She lives in Seattle, Washington, and writes nonfiction books for teens and children.

Photo Credits

Cover, pp. 1 (left, second from right), 5, 27, 29 Hemera/Thinkstock; cover, pp. 1 (second from left), 12 Andrew Harrer/Bloomberg/Getty Images; cover, pp. 1 (right), 19 Tony Avelar/Bloomberg/Getty Images; cover (background), interior graphics © www.istockphoto.com/suprun; p. 8 Neilson Barnard/Getty Images for Teen Vogue; p. 11 Ethan Miller/Getty Images; p. 16 © Phelan Ebanhack/ZUMA Press; p. 21 Tina Stallard/Getty Images; p. 23 Photodisc/Thinkstock; p. 25 Stan Honda/AFP/Getty Images; p. 31 David S. Holloway/Getty Images; p. 33 Pixland/Thinkstock; p. 36 Comstock/Thinkstock; p. 39 Scott Barbour/Getty Images.

Designer: Nicole Russo; Editor: Bethany Bryan;
Photo Researcher: Amy Feinberg